LEGENDS
OR LIES?

UNSOLVED HISTORY

LEGENDS
OR LIES?

GARY L. BLACKWOOD

 **Marshall Cavendish**
Benchmark
New York

Marshall Cavendish Benchmark
99 White Plains Road
Tarrytown, New York 10591-9001
www.marshallcavendish.us

All Internet sites were available and accurate when this book was sent to press.

Book design by Michael Nelson

LIBRARY OF CONGRESS CATALOGING-IN-PUBLICATION DATA
Legends or lies? / by Gary L. Blackwood.
p. cm. — (Unsolved history)
Summary: "Describes several legends that have intrigued people for centuries:
the lost civilization of Atlantis, the Amazons, King Arthur, St. Brendan,
Pope Joan, and El Dorado"—Provided by publisher.
Includes bibliographical references and index.
ISBN 0-7614-1891-1
1. Legends. 2. Geographical myths. I. Title. II. Series.
GR78.B53 2005
398.2'09—dc22
2004027933

Illustrations provided by Rose Corbett Gordon, Art Editor, Mystic CT, from the following sources:
Front cover: Erich Lessing/Art Resource, NY Back cover: Walker Art Gallery, Liverpool, Merseyside, UK/ Bridgeman Art Library Page i: The Pierpont Morgan Library/Art Resource, NY; pages iii, 2, 16, 24, 34, 40, 42, 43, 46, 47, 53, 58: The Granger Collection, New York; pages vi, viii, 3, 5, 17, 29, 30, 33, 37: Mary Evans Picture Library; page 6: The Art Archive; pages 7, 22, 45, 55: HIP/ Art Resource, NY; pages 8, 66: Leonard de Selva/Corbis; page 11: Erich Lessing/Art Resource, NY; page 13: Bibliotheque des Arts Decoratifs, Paris/ Bridgeman Art Library; pages 14, 63: The Art Archive/ British Library; page 18: The Art Archive/ Tate Gallery London/ Eileen Tweedy; page 19: Fine Art Photographic Library/ Art Resource, NY; pages 20, 50: Bettmann/Corbis; page 21: Greenleaf Photography/Corbis; page 26: Bridgeman Art Library; page 27: John Noble/Corbis; page 32: Joslyn Art Museum, Omaha/ Bridgeman Art Library; page 38: New York Public Library/ Art Resource, NY; page 39: Private Collection/ Bridgeman Art Library; page 48: Museo del Oro, Bogota, Colombia/ Bridgeman Art Library; page 52: Galleria Cano, Bogota, Colombia/ Bridgeman Art Library; page 56: Adam Woolfitt/Corbis.

Printed in Malaysia
135642

Front cover: Portrait of Vlad IV Tzepesch, also known as Vlad the Impaler, 15th–century Romanian ruler. Painted by an anonymous German artist in the 16th century or later.
Back cover: *Sir Galahad: The Quest for the Holy Grail*, by Arthur Hughes, 1870
Half title page: Italian tarot card, made for the Visconti-Sforza family, 15th century
Title page: *The Passing of Robin Hood*, by N. C. Wyeth, 1917
Introduction, page vi: The discovery of Atlantis as pictured by a 20th-century commercial artist

Contents

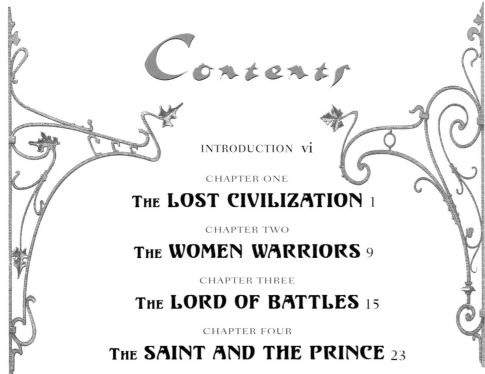

INTRODUCTION

This is, as you might expect from the title, a book about legends. It's important to note, before we go any further, that a legend is not the same thing as a myth. Although some historians make no distinction between myths and legends, considering them both a form of fantasy, most agree that there is a difference. According to author L. Sprague de Camp, the main difference is that "the former deal with gods and the latter with mortals."

It's not quite that simple, though. *The Random House Dictionary of the English Language* defines a legend as a "story handed down by tradition from earlier times and popularly accepted as historical." A myth, on the other hand, doesn't pretend to describe actual historical events. It's meant to illustrate some truth or to explain symbolically the way the world works.

As de Camp suggests, myths do usually deal with deities—the Greek god Zeus, for example, or the Indian god Shiva—or with the deeds of superheroes such as Heracles (Hercules) or

Gilgamesh. The heroes of legends sometimes display extraordinary strength or skill or cleverness, too, but they're recognizably human. Myths tend to take place at some indefinite time in the past; legends are generally set in some fairly specific, identifiable time and place.

Notice all those qualifying terms: *usually* and *sometimes*, *generally*, and *tend to*. The fact is, the dividing line between myth and legend is not always clear. Most legends contain characters or events that are clearly imaginary. And historians and archaeologists are continually finding out that some story or place or person long regarded as mythical really did exist. For example, the Greek poet Homer's tales of the Trojan War, the *Iliad* and the *Odyssey*, were considered fictional until the late nineteenth century, when the ruins of Troy were discovered.

It's not a good idea, of course, to accept a story as fact just because it's written down somewhere. Most legends were passed along by word of mouth for years, or even centuries, before they were set down on parchment or paper, and we all know from listening to rumors or jokes or urban legends how drastically a verbal account can change from one telling to the next.

But neither is it wise to dismiss a traditional tale as untrue just because it contains fanciful or exaggerated elements. No matter how distorted it may become over time, or how many layers of dubious details may be added to it, at the heart of any legend there is usually a kernel of truth. It can be difficult to find and identify, but it's worth the effort because, as scholar Richard Deacon points out, very often "legends . . . provide the only clues to what transpired before documentation began."

CHAPTER
ONE

The LOST CIVILIZATION

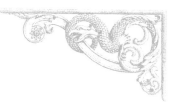

ONE OF THE MOST ANCIENT AND WIDESPREAD legends in existence involves a catastrophic flood that destroys a corrupt civilization. To us, of course, the most familiar version is the biblical story of Noah. But people all over the world have similar legends. The Mesopotamian counterpart of Noah was named Utnapishtim. In Greece, it was Deucalion. The Maya of Central America say that four hundred people survived the flood by turning into fish.

Some scientists believe that these tales may all have had their origins in an actual event. Around 9,000–10,000 BCE,* at the end of the most recent ice age, melting glaciers caused a gradual but dramatic rise in the sea level, flooding heavily populated coastal areas.

If we can believe the Greek philosopher Plato, around

Opposite: Enormous waves swamp the legendary island of Atlantis, the lost civilization whose story has been told and retold for thousands of years.

*A variety of systems of dating have been used by different cultures throughout history. Many historians now prefer to use BCE (Before Common Era) and CE (Common Era) instead of BC (Before Christ) and AD (Anno Domini), out of respect for the diversity of the world's peoples.

that same time a vast island in the middle of the Atlantic sank beneath the ocean, destroying an advanced civilization that flourished there. He called the island Atlantis.

The question is, *can* we trust Plato? If not, then the very existence of Atlantis becomes suspect, because two of Plato's works—the *Timaeus* and the *Critias,* both written around 355 BCE—are the source of nearly everything we know, or think we know, about that lost civilization.

Certainly the author did his best to make his account sound convincing, assuring his readers that "it is not invented fable but a genuine history." His source, he said, was the famed politician and poet Solon, who heard the story of Atlantis during a visit to Egypt about 600 BCE and wrote it all down for posterity. Critias, the narrator of Plato's *Critias*—and, in real life, Plato's great-grandfather—says that "these writings were in the possession of my grandfather and are actually now in mine."

Even if we accept the premise that Atlantis did exist, as Plato claims, many of the details he offers are tough to swallow. For one thing, he describes the island as "larger than Libya and Asia combined." Even if you consider that the Greeks thought Asia was

This 1785 German map indicates that remnants of Atlantis lie in the Atlantic Ocean between South America and Africa.

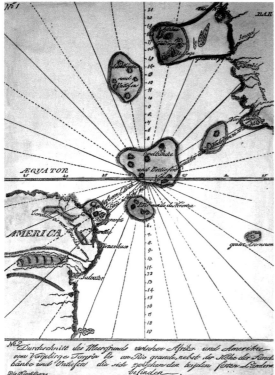

LEGENDS OR LIES?

much smaller than it really is, this seems like wild exaggeration. Plato sounds still more unreliable when he asserts that Atlantis was founded by Poseidon, the Greek god of the sea, and that its first ruler was Atlas, Poseidon's son.

Plato's account of the destruction of Atlantis is dubious, too. When the people grew corrupt and greedy, he says, the gods punished them by sending "earthquakes and floods of extraordinary violence, and in a single dreadful day and night . . . the island of Atlantis disappeared into the depths of the sea."

Another questionable element is the time period in which Atlantis supposedly flourished. In 10,000 BCE, the known world was still in the Stone Age, yet Plato's Atlanteans work with bronze, gold, and silver and build temples, canals, and bridges.

In novels such as Sir Gerald Hargreaves's *Atalanta*, Atlantis is presented as a sort of earthly paradise whose inhabitants enjoy all the pleasures of an advanced civilization.

All these fanciful details and exaggerations have made many scholars—including Plato's own pupil Aristotle—dismiss the story as fiction, a cautionary tale designed to show how a society can decay and be destroyed. But countless others, believing that no legend could survive for ten thousand years unless it had some basis in fact, have set about trying to find some vestige of the vanished island.

There are few places on Earth that have not been proposed as the site, or former site, of Atlantis, including such unlikely spots as Palestine, Great Britain, Mongolia, France, Peru, Sweden, the North and South Poles, and the Sahara.

Probably the most influential Atlantean scholar—though hardly the most credible—was Ignatius Donnelly, an eccentric American lawyer and congressman. In his 1882 book *Atlantis: The Antediluvian World*—which a later writer calls "a garbled muddle of misunderstood geology, anthropology, mythology, and linguistics"—Donnelly speculated that the Mid-Atlantic Ridge, a chain of undersea mountains, was the sunken remains of Atlantis. (In fact, the ridge was formed by molten rock welling up through the earth's crust as the tectonic plates spread apart.)

In the 1930s, psychic Edgar Cayce claimed to have learned all about Atlantis by doing "life readings" of some seven hundred individuals who had lived there during past lives. According to Cayce, the civilization dated back at least 50,000 years, and was even more technologically advanced than Plato gave it credit for. It had submarines, airplanes, television, antigravity devices, and a machine that used

crystals to harness the sun's rays. The Atlanteans, he said, brought about their own destruction by misusing this technology. Cayce considered the Bahama Islands off the coast of Florida remnants of the lost continent and predicted that, in 1968 or 1969, evidence of Atlantis would be found there.

In 1968, divers looking for that evidence made two intriguing finds: a submerged building they believed was an ancient temple, and a long, J-shaped configuration of rectangular stones that appeared to have once been a road or a wall. But a geologist who examined the "Bimini Road" dismissed it as a natural limestone formation, and another Atlantologist identified the "temple" as a storage area built by sponge divers in the 1930s.

Some scientists still consider the Bahamas a contender for the title of Atlantis. According to geologist Cesare Emiliani, during the last ice age, when sea levels were lower, the Bahamas may have consisted of a single land mass of some 40,000 square miles. But as the glaciers that covered North America melted, water came coursing down the Mississippi Valley and turned the huge island into a scattered bunch of smaller ones.

This drawing of the Mid-Atlantic Ridge appeared in a Swedish magazine in 1923. It suggests that the Azores, which lie some seven hundred miles west of Portugal, are the tip of the submerged continent of Atlantis.

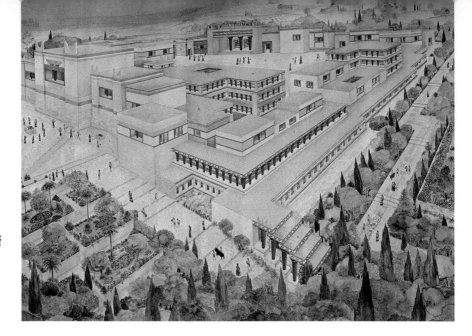

The Great Palace of Knossos on the island of Crete, as reconstructed by a modern-day artist

Probably the best known and most widely accepted Atlantis theory, though, centers around the Greek islands of Thera and Crete. In 1901, British archaeologist Sir Arthur Evans, excavating at the ancient site of Knossos on Crete, uncovered evidence of a remarkably developed culture that had existed there twenty-five centuries earlier. Later scientists found traces of this same culture on nearby Thera.

Sometime around 1500 BCE, the Minoan civilization, as Evans called it, seems to have come to a rather abrupt end. Some scientists and historians believe that the main cause was a violent volcanic eruption on Thera.

The explosion was probably ten times as powerful as the 1883 eruption of Krakatau, which was the largest in recorded history. The Thera eruption literally blew the island apart. In addition, it undoubtedly created a tsunami, a great wall of water, that would have swamped Crete; ashes from the volcano would have blanketed the ground and made growing crops impossible.

Such a catastrophe could conceivably have been the source of the Atlantis legend. The trouble is, it doesn't match the facts as recorded by Plato. It took place only a thousand years before Plato's time, not ten thousand. Crete and Thera are in the Mediterranean and Aegean Seas, not the Atlantic. And neither one is "larger than Libya and Asia combined."

Scholars who favor the Minoan theory have some ingenious solutions to those problems. According to Plato, Atlantis lay beyond the Pillars of Heracles, which is usually taken to mean the Strait of Gibraltar. But apparently the term was sometimes used to refer to Cape Matapan, which lies just northwest of Crete.

As for the disagreements about the island's size and when it was destroyed, it's been suggested that Solon, Plato's supposed source, simply made a mistake. When he was recording the story as the Egyptians told it to him, he may have misunderstood their numbering system and written down figures that were ten times too large.

The eruption on Thera blew away most of the island, then the center of the volcano collapsed, leaving a huge water-filled crater.

CHAPTER TWO

The WOMEN WARRIORS

LIKE THE STORY OF ATLANTIS, THE LEGEND OF the Amazons—a warlike race of women who lived without men—contains so many fantastic elements that for centuries it was considered just another bit of Greek mythology, in the same league as the tales about gods and superheroes.

Not even the earliest Greek poets and historians claimed to have actually met or fought against an Amazon. The heyday of the women warriors seemed to have been during the Bronze Age, a thousand years or so before they first appeared in Greek literature, sometime in the eighth or ninth century BCE. In his epic poem the *Iliad*, Homer mentions in passing "the Amazons, who go to war like men," as though he expects his readers to be familiar with them.

Opposite: According to legend, the Amazons could "ride, shoot, throw the javelin," and fight as well men, whom they preferred to live without.

And most Greeks probably were, from hearing tales about the Twelve Labors of Heracles. One of the mythical hero's supposedly impossible tasks is to obtain the girdle of Hippolyta, queen of the Amazons. (This may have been a piece of battle gear, worn to protect the stomach.)

Heracles sails to Hippolyta's capital city of Themiscyra, on the eastern shores of the Black Sea, kills her, snatches the girdle, and returns to Greece with a large number of Amazon captives. The remaining women form an alliance with a nomadic tribe called the Scythians and attack Athens but are defeated by the Greeks.

In the fifth century BCE, the Greek writer Herodotus treated the story of the Amazons not as myth but as legitimate history. In his version, Greek soldiers attack Themiscyra and sail off "with as many Amazons on board as they had succeeded in taking alive." But the women overpower and kill their captors; then, unable to navigate the ships, they drift into the Sea of Azov, north of the Black Sea, and land in Scythian territory.

After taming a band of wild horses, they begin raiding the Scythians, who mistake them for young men. Once the Scythian warriors learn the truth, they're less interested in fighting the women than in marrying them. At first the Amazons are contemptuous: "We are riders; our business is with the bow and the spear . . . but in your country no woman has anything to do with such things. . . . We could not possibly agree."

They finally give in, but only on the condition that they

This relief, sculpted on the side of a sarcophagus, or stone coffin, depicts Greek soldiers doing battle with warrior women. It dates from the fourth century BCE.

can wear men's clothing and continue to hunt and make war. This mingling of Scythians and Amazons, Herodotus says, was the origin of the Sauromatian people. The Sauromatians were still around in the fifth century BCE and, according to a contemporary of Herodotus, "their women . . . ride, shoot, throw the javelin . . . and fight with their enemies."

The Amazon attack on Athens that appears in the Heracles myth is also dealt with by Herodotus, and by a number of other chroniclers, as though it were historical fact. In his *Life of Theseus,* written about 100 CE, Plutarch says that the story "may be sufficiently confirmed by the names that the places hereabout yet retain, and the graves and monuments of those that fell in the battle."

But other scholars were already beginning to doubt that the Amazons ever existed. New elements had crept into the story that were, in the words of the historian Strabo, "marvellous and beyond belief." With each century that passed, the legend accumulated more far-fetched details: the Amazons were man haters who killed or crippled all their male children; they were cannibals; they burned off the right breast to make it easier to shoot a bow and throw a spear; they invaded and conquered Atlantis; they left Asia and settled in South America (see chapter 7).

By the twentieth century, historians were seriously suggesting that the Greeks imagined the whole thing, that their opponents may have *looked* like women but were in fact long-haired, clean-shaven men wearing kilts. Even scholars who accepted the notion of warlike women weren't inclined to take the accounts of Herodotus and the other ancient writers literally. They thought it more likely that the Amazon legend was pieced together from various unrelated reports of women who fought alongside their men in battle.

But then archaeologists in Russia began uncovering evidence that the Greeks knew what they were talking about. The first hints actually surfaced in the late nineteenth century, when Count Bobrinsky, a Russian scholar, began digging up burial mounds in the Ukraine. Inside them he found spears, knives, and arrowheads, which indicated that warriors were buried there. Most of the skeletons in the mounds, however, were female. In the fifth or sixth century BCE, the area had been occupied by the Scythians—the very people who, according to Herodotus, warred with and then wedded the Amazons.

Since Brobinsky's discovery, dozens of similar burial sites

have been unearthed in the area. Some of the women's remains showed evidence of battle wounds; one skull had an arrowhead embedded in it. Next to another skeleton was an iron-studded battle girdle. These graves and their contents seemed to provide, in the words of

author Lyn Webster Wilde, "clear and undeniable evidence that there were women warriors living in the steppe regions north of the Black Sea during Classical Greek times."

One Amazon supposedly boasted, "No mortal man begat me, but the Lord of War. Therefore my might is more than any man's."

Burial mounds were also excavated a thousand miles to the east, in territory once occupied by the Sauromatians—the race that supposedly resulted from the intermarriage of Scythians and Amazons. A fourth of the graves that contained weapons also contained the bones of women. The skeleton of one teenaged girl had bowed leg bones, suggesting that she had grown up riding horseback.

American scientist Jeannine Davis-Kimball, who worked on the excavations, believes that these Sauromatian women "held a unique position in society. They seem to have controlled much of the wealth . . . rode horseback, and possibly hunted. . . . When their territory or possessions were threatened, they took to their saddle, bows and arrows ready, to defend their animals, pastures and clan."

france morust Albanie oy kont hirlond f

The LORD OF BATTLES

PERHAPS NO LEGEND HAS BEEN RETOLD AS many times, or changed so much in the telling, as the story of Britain's greatest hero, King Arthur. The version most familiar to us today—with its chivalrous knights in gleaming armor, the Sword in the Stone, the Round Table, Camelot, the Holy Grail, Queen Guinevere, Lancelot, and the traitorous Mordred—is mainly a product of the Middle Ages, in particular the twelfth and thirteenth centuries, when there actually were armored knights and a code of chivalry.

British prime minister Winston Churchill once declared that the legend "is all true, or it ought to be." But most historians agree that the real Arthur—who, if he lived at all, probably lived in the fifth or sixth century, not the twelfth or thirteenth—would have borne very little resemblance to the medieval picture of him.

Opposite: In this illustration from a manuscript written in 1325, Arthur is depicted as a Christian knight in fourteenth-century armor.

Though Merlin is often pictured as a medieval wizard or magician, he is probably based on Myrddin, a sixth-century Welshman variously described as a bard, a prophet, or a Druid priest.

For one thing, he probably wasn't a king. That misconception comes from the extremely popular—and largely fictional—*Historia Regum Britanniae* ("History of the Kings of Britain"), written around 1135 by a Welsh teacher and clergyman named Geoffrey of Monmouth. Geoffrey also invented, or at least introduced, a number of other fanciful elements, including the wizard Merlin; the isle of Avalon, where the dying Arthur is taken; and the notion that Mordred was Arthur's nephew.

Geoffrey claimed that he used as his source "a certain very ancient book written in the British [Welsh] language." But if such a book ever existed, there's no other record of it. Before Geoffrey's time, references to Arthur are few and far between.

He's first mentioned by name in the Welsh poem *Y Gododdin*, written around 600. It praises the deeds of some other hero, but admits that "he was not Arthur." Records from this same time period show that royal families had begun naming their sons Arthur, presumably after the legendary leader. But nothing more appears about the man himself for another two centuries.

The *Historia Brittonum*, probably written about 800 by the Welsh monk Nennius, tells how the Saxons,

LEGENDS OR LIES?

a Germanic tribe, invaded Britain and how "Arthur fought against them . . . with the Kings of the Britons." He doesn't call Arthur a king, only "the leader of the battles." Nennius lists twelve of those battles, including one at Mount Badon where "nine hundred and sixty men fell . . . from a single charge of Arthur's."

A century and a half later the battle of Badon gets mentioned again, in the *Annales Cambriae* ("Annals of Wales"),

which puts the event in the year 516. Listed under the year 537 is "the Battle of Camlann, in which Arthur and Medraut [Mordred] fell."

Of course, the *Annales Cambriae* was compiled four hundred years after the fact. How can we be sure it's reliable? Let's take a look at what historians know for certain about early Britain and see how these few details about Arthur fit in.

When a Roman army under the command of Julius Caesar invaded Britain in 54 BCE, the island was occupied mainly by two cultures, the Picts in the far north and the Britons in the south. It took a century or so, but eventually the Romans conquered the Britons. Under Roman rule

Romantic novelists and poets provided Arthur with a magical sword called Excalibur, given to him by the mysterious Lady of the Lake.

southern Britain enjoyed three hundred years of relative prosperity and peace.

But by the late fourth century CE, the country was under frequent attack by Picts from the north, by Scots (who had not yet settled in present-day Scotland) from Ireland in the west, and by Saxons from the east. Meanwhile, the Roman territory of Gaul (now France) was being overrun by other German tribes. Even Rome itself was in danger.

In order to protect their empire in Europe, Roman troops were forced to withdraw from Britain, leaving the inhabitants to deal with the ruthless invaders as best they could. Unable to defend themselves against all the tribes that threatened them, the Britons made an alliance with the Saxons, promising them land in return for their help fighting the Picts and Scots.

The original Welsh name of Arthur's queen was Gwenhwyfar, which probably meant something like "white spirit."

The tactic worked. Unfortunately, the Saxons weren't content with a little land; they wanted it all. In 442 they launched a savage revolt that brought about, according to one chronicler of the time, "the general destruction of everything good and the general growth of everything evil throughout the land."

The desperate Britons rallied around a military leader named Artorius—the Welsh equivalent is Arthur—who was given the title of

LEGENDS OR LIES?

In a curious mixture of legends, some writers have speculated that the magical isle to which Arthur was transported was in fact the lost continent of Atlantis.

dux bellorum, lord of battles. Around 500 he and his men routed the Saxons at the siege of Mount Badon. Some historians believe that the main reason for the Britons' victory was that they used mounted cavalry against the Saxons, who fought on foot.

The defeat halted the advance of the Saxons; it was at least thirty years before they became a serious threat again. It may have been during this second revolt that Arthur fought one last battle against them, as recorded in the *Annales Cambriae,* and was mortally wounded.

According to the medieval version of the story, of course, he didn't actually die. As the twelfth-century writer Gerald of Wales put it, "the legends . . . encouraged us to believe that there was something otherworldly about his ending, that he resisted death and had been spirited away to some far-distant spot"—the isle of Avalon, some said,

WITHIN SIGHT OF GLASTONBURY is another location long associated with Arthur: the ruins of Cadbury Castle, an ancient hill fort.

Arthur's PALACE

Writer John Leland noted in 1542 that folk who lived in the neighborhood knew it as Camalat, "sometime a famous town or castle," and that "they have heard say Arthur much resorted to Camalat."

In 1966, a group called the Camelot Research Committee began excavating the site. In the area traditionally known as Arthur's Palace, workers discovered the foundation of a great hall, sixty by thirty feet, that dated from about 470, plus the remains of a stone and timber wall sixteen feet thick and three-quarters of a mile long. These findings are proof that, in the words of one archaeologist, "somebody, clearly a British chieftain of great status, fortified Cadbury Castle in the fifth century."

The local people have no doubt who that chieftain was. According to legend, on nights when there's a full moon the ghosts of Arthur and his men can be seen riding about on the hill. It's even rumored that someone once picked up a silver shoe cast off by one of the spectral horses.

"A surprising number of times," write scholars Peter James and Nick Thorpe, "archaeology has confirmed legends, remote and fanciful though they may have seemed."

Clouds of mystery surround the hill on which Glastonbury Abbey stood, not unlike the mists of time that shroud the death of King Arthur. Might Glastonbury have been the real Avalon?

where he sleeps until Britain has need of him again.

In 1190 the notion of the "once and future king" was challenged, when monks at Glastonbury Abbey in southwest England unearthed a skeleton of larger than normal size, enclosed in a coffin made from a hollowed-out oak tree. Beneath the coffin they found a lead cross. Several centuries later a scholar made a sketch of the cross and the words carved on it: HIC IACET SEPULTUS INCLITUS REX ARTURIUS IN INSULA AVALONIA ("Here lies buried the renowned King Arthur in the isle of Avalon"). In the mid-1500s the abbey was vandalized, and the bones were lost.

It's possible that the whole thing was a hoax, designed to lure pilgrims and their money to the abbey. The inscription does seem a bit suspicious, considering that Arthur wasn't a king and that Glastonbury isn't an island. However, during the Middle Ages the hill on which the abbey sat was surrounded by marshes, making it a sort of island.

In any case, it's doubtful that the monks created the lead cross themselves. The shape of the letters, as shown in the drawing, indicates that they were carved far earlier than 1190—perhaps as long ago as the sixth century.

est belua in mari que grece aspido delone dicitū Apr̄
latine ū aspido testudo. Cete etiam dicta. ob̄ b̄̄e
immanitate corporis. est enī sicut ille q̄ excepit

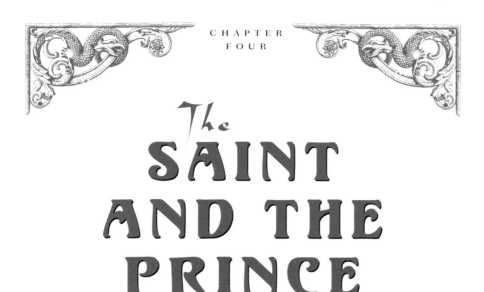

The SAINT AND THE PRINCE

WHEN GEOFFREY OF MONMOUTH AND OTHER medieval writers told of how the wounded Arthur was spirited off to the isle of Avalon, they certainly didn't have Glastonbury Abbey in mind. They made it clear that Avalon, like Atlantis, was reached by sailing west from the Pillars of Heracles.

Their picture of Avalon bears a strong resemblance to Tir na Nog (the Land of Youth), an enchanted island of Irish mythology where the weather is always springlike, and peace and happiness reign. When Christianity spread to Ireland in the fifth and sixth centuries CE, the story of Tir na Nog underwent a subtle change. The fabled Land of Youth became the Isle of the Blest, also called the Promised Land of the Saints, and only persons of great virtue could travel there.

Opposite:
Saint Brendan is said to have sought the Isle of the Blest in three epic sea voyages during which he met many adventures, like this one with a sea monster.

23

Some scholars suggest that the "monster" Brendan and his monks came upon at sea may have been a killer whale.

Of course, anyone who expected to sail across the Atlantic had to be more than just virtuous. Such a long, hazardous trip required an expert sailor and navigator. The sixth-century Irish monk Brendan—later Saint Brendan—apparently fit the bill. There's a legend that says he made three epic sea voyages in search of the Isle of the Blest.

Like most legends, this one was passed along by word of mouth for many years. It appeared in written form in three ninth-century works: the *Life of St. Malo, The Life of Brendan,* and the *Navigatio Sancti Brendani Abbatis* (Voyage of Saint Brendan the Abbot).

There's no question that Brendan was an actual historical figure, or that he was an accomplished seaman. He founded several monasteries in Ireland, including the one at Clonfert, in County Galway, from which he set out on his first Atlantic voyage around 540. He had already sailed as far as Scotland, Wales, and Brittany (part of present-day France)—fairly ambitious trips, considering the unsophisticated sort of craft he would have used.

As described in the *Navigatio,* the Irish curragh was "a light boat ribbed with wood"; the builders "covered it with ox-hides tanned with the bark of oak and smeared all the joints of the hides on the outside with fat. . . . They also placed a mast in the middle of the boat and a sail."

An abbot named Barrind visited Clonfert and told Brendan of a journey he'd made to the Isle of the Blest. Unfortunately, during the trip his boat was constantly surrounded by fog or darkness, so Barrind had no idea how to find the place again.

Inspired by the tale, Brendan convinced fourteen of his fellow monks to help him search for the Promised Land. They visited a number of curious islands, including one with sheep "so numerous that the ground could not be seen at all," and one that proved to be the back of an enormous fish. After seven years they returned home without finding the Isle of the Blest.

Undaunted, they set out again and sailed aimlessly for seven more years, discovering an island where a savage blacksmith flung burning cinders at them, and a pillar made of crystal. On their third voyage they managed to sail straight to the Promised Land. After fourteen years of searching, their visit, as recounted in the *Navigatio,* is strangely anticlimactic. Brendan and his men "took what fruit they wanted and drank from the wells," then wan-

One of the more fanciful episodes of the *Navigatio* has Brendan encountering Judas Iscariot, the apostle who betrayed Christ.

dered about until they met a young man who told them to return home.

Modern researchers have noted how closely some of the islands in the *Navigatio* resemble real places. The island of sheep was surely one of the Faeroe Islands (whose name means Sheep Islands); the burning cinders may have come not from an angry blacksmith but from a volcano, which suggests that the monks were near Iceland; the crystal pillar sounds very much like an iceberg.

These three landmarks—the Faeroes, Iceland, and fields of icebergs—are all located in the North Atlantic, along what is sometimes called "the stepping-stone route"

26

A medieval chronicler named Dicuil wrote in 825 CE that Irish monks had been living on the Faeroe Islands for nearly a century.

between Europe and America. In the tenth century, Viking settlers worked their way westward along this route, establishing colonies in Iceland and Greenland, making several voyages to Vinland—some unidentified part of North America—and settling briefly in Newfoundland.

If Brendan did that same sort of island-hopping, he could easily have ended up in the New World as well—nearly five hundred years before the Vikings. It's likely that other monks from Ireland followed his lead. According to the old Norse sagas, when the Vikings arrived in Iceland and Greenland and Vinland, they found evidence that the Irish had been there before them. They even called the unexplored area beyond Vinland "Great Ireland."

In any case, there's no doubt that Brendan's travels fired the imaginations of later explorers, including Columbus. Tim Severin, who sailed a curragh across the Atlantic in 1976 to prove it could be done, believes that the Brendan legend "helped to demolish the mentality of a closed world [and] encouraged men of learning to think of a great western land."

A legend that originated in Wales tells of one adventurer who was so inspired by tales of a new land that he led an expedition there, beating Columbus by about three centuries. According to tradition, Madoc was the son of a Welsh king named Owain Gwynedd—and, some said, a direct descendant of King Arthur.

Although Madoc reached North America nearly two centuries after the Vikings, his exploits—if they're true—are more impressive. For one thing, he explored far more of the continent. For another, he may have found a new route across the Atlantic. And unlike the Norse, whose settlement at L'Anse-aux-Meadows in Newfoundland was short-lived, Madoc and his men supposedly remained in the New World.

Many historians have dismissed all this as wishful thinking, a feeble attempt by Welsh bards to give their countrymen credit for some important discovery. But there's a good deal of evidence that, as with most legends, the story of Madoc is based on real people and events.

Owain Gwynedd was an actual person who ruled northwestern Wales for over thirty years and defended his country against the Normans who had conquered England a century earlier. Welsh bard and historian Ieuan Brechfa, writing three hundred years after the fact, claimed that "Madoc was the outcast son of Owain, and commanded by his father to be slain at birth," but that he was rescued by his mother.

After Owain died in 1170, his sons quarreled violently over who would succeed him. According to sixteenth-century writer Richard Hakluyt, Madoc "left the land in contentions betwixt his brethren and prepared certain ships with men and munition and sought adventures by seas, sailing west . . . to a land unknown."

Madoc's ship was called the *Gwennan Gorn;* a second vessel, the *Pedr Sant,* was captained by his brother Rhiryd. The vessels were most likely wooden, similar to those built by the Vikings, with a single mast and a square sail. In port records of the time, under the year 1171, both ships are listed as missing at sea.

Owain Glyndwr, the fourteenth-century Welsh rebel, followed in the spirit of Owain Gwynedd by fighting against his English overlords. Neither leader was able to successfully defend his nation's freedom.

Hakluyt implies that, rather than taking the established "stepping-stone route," Madoc headed south from Wales, in which case he could have followed the ocean currents westward. Just where the expedition ended up is a matter of dispute. Dozens of sites have been suggested, from Newfoundland to South America. But Sir

Both medieval European texts and Cherokee tales support the view that Madoc and his fellow Welshmen sailed to North America and ended up in what is now the southern part of the United States.

Thomas Herbert, a seventeenth-century scholar, states that "after long saile and no less patience . . . they descried land in the Gulph of Mexico, not farre from Florida." And if the ships were carried along by the North Equatorial Current, that's where it would have taken them.

The Welshmen may have gone ashore at Mobile Bay, in what is now Alabama, then moved inland where, according to Herbert, they "fortified some advantagious places." Archaeologists have discovered three stone for-tifications in Alabama, Tennessee, and Georgia that were built centuries before the arrival of Columbus. The Cherokee Indians who once lived in the area claimed that the walls were built by the "moon-eyed people"—men with fair skin, blond hair, and blue eyes. If Madoc and his men went to the trouble of building forts, they must have felt threatened by the native people, perhaps so threatened that they moved on.

In Kentucky, tradition has it that the Welshmen came down the Ohio River and settled for a time at the Falls of the Ohio, near present-day Louisville, but ended up battling hostile Indians again. Many of Madoc's men were killed; the rest fled northward, up the Mississippi and Missouri rivers. The story may be more than just tradition. In 1799, six skeletons with brass breastplates were reportedly dug up at the Falls of the Ohio; on the breastplates was a coat of arms with a Welsh inscription.

WHAT BECAME OF THE WELSHMEN who escaped the attack at the Falls of the Ohio? Why didn't later settlers come upon their descendants?

Perhaps they did. As far as we know, there were no Welsh *women* on the expedition, so in order to produce descendants, the men would have had to find wives among the native peoples. And some historians believe that's just what happened.

The Mandan koorig shows a clear resemblance to the modern Welsh corwg, pictured on the opposite page.

From the sixteenth century to the nine-teenth, scores of explorers, settlers, missionaries, and travelers encountered what they called "White Indians," that is, Indians who showed signs of European ancestry: pale skin, beards, blue eyes, blond or red hair. (See "The Lost Colony" in *Enigmatic Events*.) A surprising number of them report-edly spoke Welsh, some quite fluently.

Madoc and the MANDANS

For example, in 1660 a shipwrecked Welsh sailor was taken in by a Native American tribe whose language closely resembled his native tongue, and who informed him that their ancestors had come from a country called Gwynedd (as in Owain Gwynedd, Madoc's father), in Prydain Fawr (Great Britain).

In a Washington, DC, hotel in 1801, Welsh-born Lieutenant Joseph Roberts struck up a conversation with an Indian chief whose forefathers "had come from a far-distant country . . . over great waters." The Indian, Roberts said, "knew better Welsh than I did."

The chief was apparently one of the Osage people, who occupied western Missouri. But a Welsh connection has been attributed to at least a dozen other tribes in locations all over North America, from New York to British Columbia. The native people most closely scrutinized for signs of European ancestry were the Mandan, who lived along the upper Missouri River in the mid-1800s.

George Catlin, the noted artist of the American West, lived among the Mandan for eight years. Many of the portraits he painted of them clearly show European features. Catlin also observed that their round, skin-covered boats, which they called *koorig*, were identical to the Welsh coracle, or *corwg*.

He cataloged hundreds of other words and phrases that were similar in Mandan and Welsh. Perhaps the most striking example was a Mandan prayer to the Great Spirit: *Madoc Maho Paneta am byd*. The closest Welsh equivalent would be *Madoc Mawr penadur am byth*, which means "Great Madoc, Sovereign forever."

Both the Indian and Welsh vessels are rounded and covered with animal skins.

The POPESS

POPE JOAN, THE NINTH-CENTURY WOMAN
who purportedly posed as a man and became head of the
Catholic Church, doesn't have much in common with the
heroes of other legends. Although she was a cleric, like
Brendan, she made no epic voyages and discovered no
new lands. And although she wore men's clothing, like the
Amazons, it was because she wanted to be a scholar, not
a warrior.

The most significant difference between her legend and
the others is that hers didn't depend on word of mouth for
its survival. She was first mentioned in writing by
Anastasius Bibliothecarius, custodian of the papal library, a
contemporary of Joan's who presumably knew her person-
ally. Why, then, is she considered a legend and not a
documented historical figure?

Opposite: "Despite
all attempts to kill
her off, Pope Joan
keeps cropping
up"—even in such
unlikely places as
this fifteenth-century
tarot card.

35

Well, apparently her story *was* thought to be fact for at least six hundred years. No particular attempt was made to deny it until the Protestant Reformation of the sixteenth century, when Protestants began using the scandalous notion of a woman pope as a way to discredit the Catholic Church.

It wasn't all that novel an idea, actually. There were earlier examples of cross-dressing clerics, including the fourth-century hermit Pelagius, who was discovered at death to be a woman; she was later declared a saint (and given a feminine name, Pelagia). In the fifth century, Euphrosyne, another future saint, supposedly disguised herself as a man and entered a monastery in order to escape an arranged marriage. Such tales very likely inspired Joan to undertake her audacious deception.

Her origins are uncertain. The best guess is that she was born around 818 to English missionaries in Germany. The name Joan—the female version of her papal name, John—may have been attached to her after her death. Various sources have recorded her real name as Agnes, Gilberta, Margaret, or Jutt. At the age of twelve, it's said, she fell in love with a monk and, disguising herself as a man, entered the monastery to be with him. Eventually she was found out and fled to Athens where, still posing as a man, she pursued an education.

In time she moved on to Rome. Thanks to her eloquence and her knowledge of the scriptures, she became a cardinal and a favorite of Pope Leo IV. When Leo died in

855, Joan was unanimously elected his successor.

There's no mention of Joan or her papal name, John VIII, in the pontificals, or "pope books," for the time (although a later pope also called himself John VIII). But there is an account of an unnamed pontiff whose background sounds suspiciously similar. When it was announced that he had been elected, he became frightened and tried to refuse the honor—just the sort of reaction an impostor like Joan might have.

Pope Leo IV reigned from 847 to 855. Since Catholic clergy were allowed to marry at the time, one historian speculates that Joan may have been Leo's wife.

Several chroniclers of the eleventh and twelfth centuries referred briefly to Joan, but the first to cover her career in detail was Martin Polonus, who wrote in his 1265 work *Chronicon Pontificum et Imperatum* ("Chronicle of the Popes and Emperors") that she was pope for "two years, five months and four days." Unfortunately, "she became pregnant by the person with whom she was intimate. But not knowing the time of her delivery, while going from Saint Peter's to the Lateran [Church] . . . she brought forth a child. . . . And afterwards dying, she was, it is said, buried

This painting, depicting Joan's delivery of a child in the street, illustrates a 15th-century manuscript. Joan's story captivated a wide audience for hundreds of years prior to the Protestant Reformation.

in that place." According to Polonus, the child, a son, survived and became a bishop.

The site was marked by a memorial—some sources say it was a slab of stone with an inscription; others say it was a statue—and the route was named the Vicus Papissa ("The Street of the Woman Pope"). Around 1590, Pope Sixtus V reportedly had the memorial torn down and thrown into the Tiber River.

Another statue labeled "Pope John VIII, a woman from England" supposedly sat among the papal busts in Siena Cathedral for hundreds of years; in the sixteenth century it was either removed or renamed (and perhaps altered to look more manly).

It sounds as though the Catholic Church was bent on erasing all record of the woman pope, perhaps in response to the embarrassing accusations of the Protestants. If so, the campaign was only partly successful. Joan's story, which had once been widely accepted as true, came to be regarded as apocryphal. But it certainly didn't fade away, as the church no doubt hoped it would. "Despite all attempts to kill her off," writes author Peter Stanford, "Pope Joan keeps cropping up."

She appears as La Papesse on one of the cards in some tarot decks, which are used to tell fortunes; her card usually represents intuition and inspiration. She also inspired a card game called Pope Joan that was popular in Victorian England. She's been the subject of countless stage plays,

A Present for a Papist:
OR THE
LIFE and DEATH
OF
POPE JOAN,
Plainly Proving
Out of the Printed Copies, and
Manuscripts of Popish Writers and
others, that a Woman called
JOAN, was really
POPE of ROME;
And was there Deliver'd of a Bastard
Son in the open Street, as She went
in Solemn Procession.

By a LOVER of TRUTH;
Denying Human Infallibility.

LONDON,
Printed for T. D. and are to be sold at
the Ship in St. Mary Axe, and by
most Booksellers, 1675.

The title page of a 1675 Protestant pamphlet expresses shock and outrage at the Roman Catholic Church.

poems, novels, and films—even a successful musical. Stanford explains the stubborn survival of her legend—and perhaps all the legends recounted here—this way: "People believe in her and go on believing in her because they want her to have happened."

The OUTLAW

ON NEARLY ANYONE'S LIST OF THE GREATEST and most familiar British heroes, King Arthur would rank number one, with Robin Hood a distant second. But considering that Arthur had at least a seven-hundred-year head start on him, the outlaw of Sherwood Forest has done pretty well for himself. Historian John Bellamy calls him "the most memorable figure in the whole history of medieval England."

The fact that his adventures have been so popular for so long and have been retold so many times does create problems for researchers, though. Like the Arthur legend, the tales of Robin Hood have accumulated layer upon layer of invention and embellishment (such as Maid Marian, or the notion that Robin stole from the rich and gave to the poor), until we've totally lost sight of the historical figure who inspired them.

Opposite: Robin Hood is said to have lived with his merry men in Sherwood Forest in Nottinghamshire, England. Many place-names there, such as Robin Hood's Bay and Robin Hood's Cave, still bear his name.

In most books and films, Robin is not a desperate fugitive but a dashing, romantic figure. This painting of Robin with Maid Marian at a tournament was created by N. C. Wyeth for a 1917 book.

Naturally there are a lot more written records in existence from Robin Hood's time—which was most likely the thirteenth or fourteenth century—than there are from Arthur's. You might think that would make it easier to track down the elusive outlaw. But what it really does is give us too many possibilities to choose from—especially if we assume that Robin was a nickname for Robert. Documents of the time list a dismaying number of Robert Hoods, or some variation. Of course, there's also the chance that Robin Hood was just an alias, which opens up even more possibilities.

Scholars are fairly certain that, if there was an actual outlaw by that name, he lived before the 1370s, since William Langland's poem *Piers Plowman,* written in that decade, refers to "rymes of Robyn Hode" as if the man were already a legend.

The lengthy ballad *A Gest* [tale] *of Robin Hood* was probably written in the late fourteenth century, too. It introduced the idea that Robin "was a good outlawe, / And dyde pore men moch god." Although it's likely that a lot of the work is fictional, the *Gest* is a valuable source. One scholar calls it "the original and perhaps the only genuine written account of the exploits of Robin Hood and his band."

The first writer to treat the outlaw as a historical figure was Andrew de Wyntoun, whose 1420 chronicle of Scotland has Robin Hood pursuing his trade in the year 1283. John Major, author of the 1521 work *Historia Majoris Britanniae* ("History of Greater Britain"), preferred a date around 1190: "About this time . . . there flourished those most famous robbers Robert Hood, an Englishman, and Little John, who lay in wait in the woods but spoiled of their goods those only that were wealthy."

Nearly a century went by before anyone tried to actually identify the man behind the name. The *Gest* makes it clear that Robin is not a common criminal but a gentleman. Sixteenth-century playwright Anthony Munday was more specific; he suggested that the outlaw was, in fact, the rightful Earl of Huntington. William Stukeley, an eighteenth-century doctor and parson, drew up a family tree for "Robert Fitzooth, commonly called Robin Hood, pretended earl of Huntington" that traced his heritage back to William the Conqueror. Aside from this highly questionable

Little John may have been an actual historical figure. A 1318 document mentions a robber named John le Litel; in 1323, a certain "Littel John" was accused of poaching deer.

document, there's no real evidence to support the Huntington theory.

Although the *Gest* isn't much help in the matter of Robin's identity, it does hint at a time frame by telling us who was on England's throne: "Edwarde our comly [handsome] kynge." Unfortunately, we have several of those to choose from, too: Edward I, who ruled England from 1272 to 1307; his son Edward II, who took over the throne from 1307 to 1327; or *his* son Edward III, who was king from 1327 to 1377.

Around 1838, Joseph Hunter, assistant keeper of London's Public Record Office, began examining documents from the reign of Edward II. He discovered references to a Robert Hode in the records of the manor of Wakefield in southern Yorkshire—traditional Robin Hood territory. Hode is last mentioned in November 1317, when he's fined for failing to show up for military duty in the king's army.

Hunter speculated that Hode may have joined the forces of the Earl of Lancaster, who was leading a rebellion against Edward II. After Lancaster was defeated and beheaded in 1322, many of his supporters became outlaws. Interestingly enough, the livery (clothing of a distinctive color) worn by Lancaster's followers was Lincoln green—the very shade supposedly favored by Robin Hood and his men.

Hunter also found that, in 1323, King Edward visited Sherwood and Barnsdale—the royal forests where Robin

Hood hides out in the legends—to investigate the poaching of deer. This is one of the events recounted in the *Gest*.

According to the ballad, Robin was pardoned by the king and entered royal service for a year. "Now it will scarcely be believed," wrote Hunter, "but it is nevertheless the plain and simple truth that in documents . . . containing accounts of expenses in the king's household we find the name of 'Robyn Hode' not once but several times occurring, receiving . . . the pay of 3d [pence] a day" as one of Edward's personal servants.

Although this 1324 royal account book is unreadable to most of us, it lists "Robyn Hode" as a porter of the king's chamber.

The accounts show that he was in the king's service until November of 1324—about a year from the time of Edward's visit to Sherwood and Barnsdale. This matches very closely the story as told in the *Gest*.

Hunter and other scholars have concluded that Robert Hode of Wakefield, Robyn Hode, the king's manservant, and the Robin Hood of legend were all the same person. But, like most theories, this one is far from being unanimously

ENGLAND IS POSITIVELY PACKED WITH SITES that purport to have some Robin Hood connection. There's Robin Hood's Field, Robin Hood's Cave, Robin Hood's Cross, Robin Hood's Well, Robin Hood's

Robin Hood's GRAVE

Bay, and any number of Robin Hood's Butts (a reference not to his anatomy but to spots he may have used as archery targets). The most intriguing site, though, and the one that most strongly suggests he was an actual person, is Robin Hood's grave.

Sixteenth-century chronicler Richard Grafton told the story of how the outlaw met his end. Robin, "troubled with sicknesse, came to a certein Nonry [nunnery] in Yorkshire called Bircklies [Kirklees Abbey, near Wakefield], where desirying to be let blood, he was betrayed and bled to deth. After whose death the Prioresse of the same place caused him to be buried by the high way side. . . . And at either end of the sayde Tombe was erected a crosse of stone, which is to be seene there at this present." Some say the prioress was prompted to do the deed by one of Robin's old enemies, Roger of Doncaster.

In 1665 scholar Nathaniel Johnston made a drawing of the outlaw's tomb and the inscription on it: "here lie[s] robard hude." In the early nineteenth century, railway workers broke the stone to pieces—not out of sheer destructiveness, but because they believed that chips from Robin Hood's gravestone were a cure for toothache.

In one version of the legend, Robin shoots an arrow from the gatehouse of Kirklees Abbey and asks to be buried where the arrow falls.

accepted. Some historians point to other possible candidates, such as the Robert Hood—also known as Hobbehod—who is listed as a fugitive in census rolls from 1228 and 1230. That would mean, though, that he was around well before any of the Edwards was king, and also before the longbow, Robin Hood's weapon of choice, was in general use in England.

Some suggest that the legend, rather than being inspired by a single figure, "could well embody the adventures of several distinct

The longbow was in use in Wales early in the twelfth century, but it didn't come into its own in England until King Edward I adopted the weapon for his troops around 1280.

real outlaws all borrowing the name." Others dismiss the figure of Robin Hood as pure fancy, claiming that "the name originally belonged to a mythical forest-elf . . . and that it was afterwards applied by English ballad-writers . . . to any robber-leader who made his home in forests or moors, excelled in archery, defied the oppressive forest laws, and thus attracted popular sympathy."

Folk in the Middle Ages apparently had no doubts, though, about whether or not Robin was a real person. There's an English saying that dates back to the early 1400s: "Robin Hood in Barnsdale stood." It was used to refer to something so obviously true that it needed no discussion.

The CITY OF GOLD

ORDINARILY, ONLY HISTORIANS AND archaeologists are motivated enough to spend years tracking down the origins of legendary characters and places. But a few legends are, like the story of Saint Brendan's voyages, so compelling that people are willing to risk their lives trying to find the source. Perhaps the most compelling— and most elusive—of all is the legend of El Dorado.

Many of the explorers who sought El Dorado expected to find a city, or a whole country, where everything was made of gold. Originally, though, the term referred not to a place but to a person—*el hombre dorado.*

The tale of the Golden Man was first recorded in full in the 1620s by a Spanish monk, Pedro Simón. On the Cundinamarca plateau of northwest South America, in what is now Colombia, there was a lake called Guatavitá, where "a few times a year," according to Simón, a curious ceremony took place.

Opposite: As early as 1541, Spanish chroniclers told of a "great lord or prince" covered with "gold dust as fine as ground salt."

49

As a way of honoring the gods, the native people coated their chief "with a kind of sticky turpentine on which much fine gold dust was scattered," and rowed him into the middle of the lake where he would "make offerings by throwing emeralds and pieces of gold into the water. . . . Then, washing his body with herbs like soap, the gold on his skin fell into the water and the ceremony ended."

By the time Simón wrote this, the Spanish had already been robbing the Indians of the New World of their precious metals for a century. In 1519, Hernán Cortés entered Mexico and amassed a fantastic horde of Aztec gold. Francisco Pizarro took even greater amounts from the Incas of Peru. Their exploits opened the door for a steady stream of treasure seekers. "Gold is . . . worshipped by them as a god," wrote a Spanish monk. "They come without intermission and without thought, across the sea, to toil and danger, in order to get it."

In 1536 Pizarro's deputy in Ecuador, Sebastián de Belalcázar, heard the story of the gilded chief of Lake Guatavitá and set out with several hundred soldiers and a thousand or more Indian porters to find the place. He expected the journey to take less than two weeks.

An uneducated man who once worked as a swineherd, Francisco Pizarro became a wealthy member of the Spanish aristocracy after his conquest of Peru.

LEGENDS OR LIES?

Belalcázar wasn't aware that two other expeditions were also on their way to the Cundinamarca plateau. Seven hundred men under the command of Gonzalo Jiménez de Quesada were heading south from the town of Santa Marta on the coast of Colombia. Another group had started out in Coro, on the Venezuela coast. It was led by Nicolaus Federmann, a young German who, five years earlier, had roamed around Venezuela in an unsuccessful search for gold.

All three parties endured almost unimaginable hardships: rain so incessant that their clothing rotted away; jungle so thick that they had to hack their way through; disease-bearing mosquitoes; snakes, jaguars, crocodiles; hostile Indians with poison-tipped arrows.

Though it took Quesada ten miserable months to reach the land of El Dorado, he beat the other two expeditions. His army of seven hundred had dwindled to 166. They found that the native people, the Chibcha, were quite wealthy. But the valuable mineral to which they owed their prosperity was salt. The small amount of gold they had was obtained by trading with other tribes.

There was a lake in the area called Guatavitá, and the Chibcha had once performed a ceremony there that involved coating a chief in gold dust. But the ritual hadn't taken place for thirty or forty years. Quesada subdued the Indians, claimed the land—which he called the New Kingdom of Granada—for Spain, and built a church that was the beginning of the city of Bogotá.

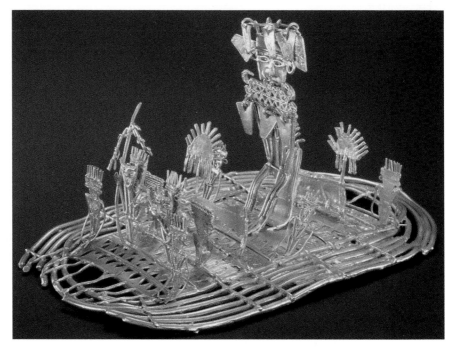

This copper and gold figurine depicting the Golden Man ceremony was retrieved from Lake Guatavitá.

Then Belalcázar's expediton turned up. The trip that was supposed to last two weeks had taken him two years. His army, too, had been reduced to just 166 men. They were disheartened, to say the least, to discover that someone else had gotten there first and confiscated what little gold there was.

Imagine the dismay of Federmann's band when it arrived a short time later, battered and weary after traversing an almost impassable mountain range to the east. Although the coincidence seems incredible, the German's remaining followers supposedly also numbered 166.

Since there was no city of gold on the plateau, Federmann and Belalcázar didn't consider it worth fighting over. The three leaders sailed home together, leaving

Quesada's brother Hernán in charge. Hernán put men to work bailing the water from Lake Guatavitá with hollow gourds, in order to recover the gold dust and emeralds on the bottom. They actually found the equivalent of about four thousand *pesos de oro*—a considerable sum, but hardly worth all the effort.

Frustrated, Hernán decided to look elsewhere for El Dorado. He led his men east, into the very area where Federmann had just wandered for three years without finding a trace of gold. After only one year the half of his party that was still alive turned back.

Although his effort was a failure, it gave others the notion that the city of gold lay in Venezuela. In 1541, Francisco Pizarro's brother Gonzalo arrived there with an expedition that was better equipped than any previous one, but just as unsuccessful. When the native people denied any knowledge of El Dorado, Gonzalo tried to torture the truth out of them. One chief cleverly got rid of the invaders by giving them a fabulous fake description of the golden city and assuring them that it lay somewhere farther east.

When Gonzalo ran low on supplies, he sent a party down the Napo River to search for food. Unable to make their way back against the strong current, the men floated into a larger river and followed it all the way to the Atlantic Ocean.

Some South American Indians regarded gold as a sacred metal that captured the energy of the sun. This golden mask, found in a grave in Peru, was made before the arrival of the Europeans.

Along the way they encountered hostile Indians. According to one Spanish soldier, a number of them were women, "very white and tall . . . with their bows and arrows in their hand, doing as much fighting as ten Indian men." Assuming that these were the fabled Amazons, who were said to have settled in South America, the Spaniards named the river after them.

In the fifty years that followed, there were at least a dozen new attempts to find the city of gold, all of them disastrous. One was led by Gonzalo Jiménez de Quesada, who thirty years earlier had hoped to find El Dorado on the Cundinamarca plateau. Quesada, now nearly seventy, set out for southern Venezuela with four hundred men and returned three years later with twenty-five. Don Pedro de Silva, a veteran of two previous failed expeditions, explored the same area in 1576, taking along his two small daughters. After Carib Indians and tropical diseases had taken their toll, there was only one man left.

In 1595, rumors of the golden city reached English explorer Sir Walter Raleigh. (For more on Raleigh, see "The Lost Colony" in *Enigmatic Events* and "The Playwright" in *Debatable Deaths*.) When he sailed for South America, he had more in mind than just finding gold; he planned to befriend the Indians, drive out the Spanish, and claim the land for England's Queen Elizabeth I.

He tried to reach El Dorado by boat, up Venezuela's Orinoco River, but was forced to give up and return home. By now, many people had begun to doubt that the city of

This 1599 map, from an account of Sir Walter Raleigh's search for El Dorado, labels the city of gold "Manoa," and places it on an island in "Lake Parimá." Although neither lake nor city existed, they continued to appear on maps for two hundred years.

gold existed at all. Undaunted, Raleigh mounted a second expedition—also a failure. In 1603 James I, England's new monarch, accused Raleigh of conspiring with the Spanish against him. Although the charges were unfounded, Raleigh spent the next twelve years in prison.

You might think this would put an end to his dreams of El Dorado. But in 1617 he convinced James to let him make one more attempt "to honor my sovereign and enrich his kingdom with gold." The king may have seen it as a chance to get rid of Raleigh without having to actually execute him.

Before the expedition even reached South America it was struck by a hurricane and by an epidemic of dysentery.

The Chibcha people believed that Lake Guatavitá was the dwelling place of a goddess who demanded gifts of gold and emeralds.

Raleigh was so ill that he had to put his nephew and his oldest son, Walter, in charge of the exploring party. In a skirmish with Spanish soldiers, Walter was killed.

"I never knew what sorrow meant till now," Raleigh mourned in a letter to his wife. "My brains are broken, and 'tis a torment to me to write." He returned to England with no gold and with only one of his original fourteen ships. Most of his men had turned pirate and gone to search not for El Dorado but for Spanish ships to prey on. Raleigh found himself charged again with treason—this time for *fighting* the Spanish, who were now supposedly at peace with England.

After Raleigh was executed in 1618, the hunt for El Dorado, which had obsessed men for nearly a century, began to lose momentum. But it didn't end altogether. In 1823 a group of investors tried again to drain Guatavitá, but managed to lower the water level only ten feet. Another company emptied the lake in 1904, but the sun turned the exposed mud as hard as concrete; the company retrieved only a few golden ornaments. In 1965, Colombia declared the lake a historical site and banned all attempts to recover the treasure of the Golden Man.

WORDS FOR THE WISE

Churchill, Sir Winston (1874–1965) Prime minister of Great Britain 1940–1945 and again 1951–1955. Churchill, a noted author and historian, was awarded the Nobel Prize for literature in 1953.

Cortés, Hernán (1485–1547) Spanish conquistador (conqueror) who participated in the conquest of Cuba and then set out to do the same in Mexico. He defeated the Aztecs with relative ease partly because the Indians were devastated by disease, and partly because he pretended to be their legendary ruler, Quetzalcoatl.

Faeroe (fair-oh) Islands A group of eighteen islands—seventeen of them inhabited—that lie about halfway between Scotland's Shetland Islands and Iceland. Now part of

Denmark, the Faeroes were inhabited by Irish monks during the 700s CE and settled by Vikings a century later.

Hakluyt (hak-loot), Richard (1552?–1616) English clergyman and writer whose books of geography and travel promoted the exploration and colonization of the New World.

Herodotus (about 484–425 BCE) Greek writer sometimes called the Father of History. His account of the Persian Wars is the first true work of history written in the Western world.

Homer Greek poet traditionally credited with composing the epic poems the *Iliad* and the *Odyssey,* probably sometime in the eighth or ninth century BCE. Many scholars believe the works were recited aloud during Homer's time and not written down until much later.

Inca A South American native people who, before the arrival of the Spanish in 1532, ruled an empire that covered much of modern-day Peru, Ecuador, and Chile, plus parts of Bolivia and Argentina.

James I (1566–1625) King of England from the death of Elizabeth I in 1603 until his own death. He was already king of Scotland, having inherited the throne from his mother, Mary, Queen of Scots, when he was less than two years old.

Langland, William (about 1330–1400) English cleric and writer whose long poem *The Vision of William Concerning Piers the Plowman* is considered one of the masterpieces of Middle English literature.

manuscript A book produced entirely by hand.

Maya A group of Native American peoples who occupied southern Mexico and Central America from at least 2000 BCE. They developed a sophisticated culture with a written language, impressive architecture—including stone pyramids that can still be seen—and a knowledge of astronomy and mathematics.

Mesopotamia The region in the Middle East between the Tigris and Euphrates rivers, where the first advanced civilization arose around 3500 BCE.

Minoans A Bronze Age people who flourished on the island of Crete from about 3000 to 1450 BCE. Their name derives from Minos, king of Knossos, known in Greek myth for the labyrinth, or maze, where he kept the Minotaur, a monster that was half man, half bull. Artwork found at Knossos features young men and women engaged in some sort of athletic contest or ceremony that involves leaping over bulls.

Pizarro, Francisco (1475?–1541) Spanish adventurer who participated in expeditions to Colombia and Panama before invading Peru in 1532. Through trickery, Pizarro captured the Inca king Atahualpa. He demanded a huge ransom for the ruler's release, then, after it was paid, he had Atahualpa killed.

plateau A relatively level area of land that lies at a higher elevation than the land around it.

Plato (about 428–347 BCE) Influential Greek writer whose works—known as dialogues because many of them feature fictional conversations between well-known historical figures—explore problems of philosophy and politics.

Plutarch (about 46–120 CE) Greek priest of Apollo, philosopher, and writer. Plutarch was best known for his biographies of Greek and Roman leaders, which furnished Shakespeare with the plots for his plays *Coriolanus, Julius Caesar,* and *Antony and Cleopatra.* Plutarch's philosophy was based on that of Plato.

Raleigh, Sir Walter (1552?–1618) English military commander and writer. A favorite courtier of Queen Elizabeth I, Raleigh incurred her displeasure by marrying one of her maids of honor. The search for El Dorado wasn't his only fiasco; in 1587 he financed an ill-fated attempt to colonize Virginia.

tarot A deck of seventy-eight cards used by fortune-tellers since at least the late fourteenth century. The fifty-six cards known as the Minor Arcana are similar to ordinary playing cards. The rest of the deck, the Major Arcana, contains symbols such as the Moon, the Wheel of Fortune, and the Hanged Man, which represent various virtues and vices.

Trojan War A ten-year conflict in which, according to legend, the Greek army laid siege to the city of Troy (in what is now western Turkey). The Greeks' original purpose was to rescue Helen, wife of the king of Sparta, who had been abducted by Paris, son of the Trojan king. Excavations at the site of Troy suggest that the story was based on real events of the thirteenth or twelfth century BCE.

TO LEARN MORE ABOUT LEGENDS

BOOKS—FICTION

Creswick, Paul. *Robin Hood*. New York: Atheneum, 1984.

A lively retelling of the legend, complete with Maid Marian, the Sheriff of Nottingham, and the Merry Men, illustrated with striking paintings by famed artist N. C. Wyeth.

White, T. H. *The Once and Future King*. New York: Putnam, 1958.

This ambitious and highly entertaining version of the King Arthur story first appeared as four separate novels: *The Sword in the Stone* (1938), *The Witch in the Wood* (1939), *The Ill-Made Knight* (1940), and *The Candle in the Wind* (1958). A companion volume, *The Book of Merlyn*, was published in 1977.

ONLINE INFORMATION

http://users.cihost.com/ata/atlantis.htm

Features a variety of articles about Atlantis, plus the complete text of Plato's account.

www.benturner.com/robinhood

An extensive, well-designed site with information about movies, books, and television shows based on the Robin Hood legend, a forum on which users can post comments, a continuing story that readers can contribute to, and lots of links to related sites.

www.davidparlett.co.uk/histocs/popejoan.html

The history of the Pope Joan card game and rules for playing it.

www.public.iastate.edu/~camelot/arthur.html
   Contains a lengthy list of King Arthur sites.

BIBLIOGRAPHY

Andronik, Catherine M. *Quest for a King: Searching for the Real King Arthur.* New York: Atheneum, 1989.

Arciniegas, Germán. *The Knight of El Dorado: The Tale of Don Gonzalo Jiménez de Quesada and His Conquest of New Granada, Now Called Colombia.* New York: Greenwood, 1968.

Aron, Paul. *Unsolved Mysteries of American History: An Eye-Opening Journey through 500 Years of Discoveries, Disappearances, and Baffling Events.* New York: Wiley, 1997.

Aron, Paul. *Unsolved Mysteries of History: An Eye-Opening Investigation into the Most Baffling Events of All Time.* New York: Wiley, 2000.

Ashe, Geoffrey. *The Discovery of King Arthur.* Garden City, NY: Doubleday, 1985.

Ashe, Geoffrey. *Land to the West: St. Brendan's Voyage to America.* New York: Viking, 1962.

Bellamy, John. *Robin Hood: An Historical Enquiry.* Bloomington, IN: Indiana University Press, 1985.

Boland, Charles Michael. *They All Discovered America.* Garden City, NY: Doubleday, 1961.

Bord, Janet, and Colin Bord. *Ancient Mysteries of Britain.* Manchester, NH: Salem House, 1986.

Brengle, Richard L., ed. *Arthur King of Britain: History, Romance, Chronicle & Criticism.* New York: Appleton-Century-Crofts, 1964.

Chapman, Walker. *The Search for El Dorado.* Indianapolis: Bobbs-Merrill, 1967.

Darrah, John. *The Real Camelot: Paganism and the Arthurian Romances.* New York: Thames and Hudson, 1981.

Day, David. *The Search for King Arthur.* New York: Facts on File, 1995.

Deacon, Richard. *Madoc and the Discovery of America: Some New Light on an Old Controversy.* New York: George Braziller, 1966.

de Camp, L. Sprague. *Lost Continents: The Atlantis Theme in History, Science, and Literature.* New York: Dover, 1970.

Editors of Reader's Digest. *Great Mysteries of the Past: Experts Unravel Fact and Fallacy Behind the Headlines of History.* Pleasantville, NY: Reader's Digest, 1991.

Editors of Reader's Digest. *Strange Stories, Amazing Facts: Stories that Are Bizarre, Unusual, Odd, Astonishing, and Often Incredible.* Pleasantville, NY: Reader's Digest, 1976.

Editors of Time-Life Books. *The Search for El Dorado.* Lost Civilizations. Alexandria, VA: Time-Life, 1994.

Ellis, Richard. *Imagining Atlantis.* New York: Knopf, 1998.

Furneaux, Rupert. *The World's Most Intriguing True Mysteries: Enthralling Accounts of Events that Continue to Mystify and Baffle.* New York: Arco, 1966.

Galanopoulos, A. G., and Edward Bacon. *Atlantis: The Truth Behind the Legend.* Indianapolis: Bobbs-Merrill, 1969.

"Georgia's Ft. Mountain and Prince Madoc of Wales." www.tylwythteg.com/fortmount/Ftmount.html

Holt, J. C. *Robin Hood.* New York: Thames and Hudson, 1982.

Hutchins, Robert Maynard, ed. *Plutarch.* Great Books of the Western World, vol. 14. Chicago: Encyclopaedia Brittanica, 1952.

Huyghe, Patrick. *Columbus Was Last.* New York: Hyperion, 1992.

James, Peter, and Nick Thorpe. *Ancient Mysteries.* New York: Ballantine, 1999.

Jenkins, Elizabeth. *The Mystery of King Arthur.* New York: Coward, McCann & Geoghegan, 1975.

Kleinbaum, Abby Wettan. *The War against the Amazons*. New York: New Press, 1983.

Knight, Stephen. *Robin Hood: A Complete Study of the English Outlaw*. Oxford: Blackwell, 1994.

Lord, Lewis. "The Lady Was a Pope: A Bestseller Revives the Outlandish Tale of Joan." www.usnews.com/doubleissue/mysteries/pope.htm

Mooney, Michael Macdonald, ed. *George Catlin: Letters and Notes on the North American Indians*. New York: Clarkson N. Potter, 1975.

Morison, Samuel Eliot. *The European Discovery of America: The Northern Voyages:* A.D. *500–1600*. New York: Oxford University Press, 1971.

Mysteries of Mind Space & Time: The Unexplained. vols. 3, 13, 17, 19. Westport, CT: H. S. Stuttman, 1992.

O'Meara, John J., trans. *The Voyage of Saint Brendan: Journey to the Promised Land*. Atlantic Highlands, NJ: Humanities Press, 1976.

Reno, Frank D. *The Historic King Arthur: Authenticating the Celtic Hero of Post-Roman Britain*. Jefferson, NC: McFarland & Co., 1996.

Severin, Tim. *The Brendan Voyage*. New York: McGraw Hill, 1978.

Stanford, Peter. *The Legend of Pope Joan: In Search of the Truth*. New York: Henry Holt, 1998.

Thorndike, Joseph J., Jr., ed. *Mysteries of the Past*. New York: American Heritage, 1977.

Trull, D. "Atlantis 'Discovery' Gets Sunk."
www.parascope.com/articles/0997/atlantis.htm

Wahlgren, Erik. *The Vikings and America*. New York: Thames and Hudson, 1986.

Wilde, Lyn Webster. *On the Trail of the Women Warriors: The Amazons in Myth and History*. New York: Thomas Dunne, 1999.

Wilson, Colin, and Damon Wilson. *The Mammoth Encyclopedia of the Unsolved*. New York: Carroll & Graf, 2000.

NOTES ON QUOTES

Introduction

Page vi, "the former deal": de Camp, *Lost Continents,* p. 233.

Page vii, "legends . . . provide": Deacon, *Madoc and the Discovery of America,* p. 237.

Chapter One: The Lost Civilization

Page 2, "it is not invented": Galanopoulos and Bacon, *Atlantis,* p. 14.

Page 2, "these writings": ibid., p. 15.

Page 2, "larger than Libya": Ellis, *Imagining Atlantis,* p. 7.

Page 3, "earthquakes and floods": James and Thorpe, *Ancient Mysteries,* p. 19.

Page 4, "a garbled muddle": Ellis, *Imagining Atlantis,* p. 43.

Chapter Two: The Women Warriors

Page 9, "the Amazons": James and Thorpe, *Ancient Mysteries,* p. 435.

Page 10, "with as many": Kleinbaum, *The War against the Amazons,* p. 6.

Page 10, "We are riders": ibid., p. 7.

Page 11, "their women . . . ride": Wilde, *On the Trail of the Women Warriors,* p. 43.

Page 11, "may be sufficiently": Hutchins, *Plutarch,* pp. 10–11.

Page 11, "marvellous and beyond": Kleinbaum, *The War against the Amazons,* p. 21.

Page 13, "clear and undeniable": Wilde, *On the Trail of the Women Warriors,* p. 63.

Page 13, "held a unique": James and Thorpe, *Ancient Mysteries,* p. 443.

LEGENDS OR LIES?

Chapter Three: The Lord of Battles

Page 15, "is all true": Brengle, *Arthur King of Britain,* p. viii.

Page 16, "a certain very": James and Thorpe, *Ancient Mysteries,* p. 459.

Page 16, "he was not": Brengle, *Arthur King of Britain,* p. 327.

Page 17, "Arthur fought against" and "the leader": Jenkins, *The Mystery of King Arthur,* p. 30.

Page 17, "nine hundred": James and Thorpe, *Ancient Mysteries,* p. 452.

Page 17, "the Battle of Camlann": Brengle, *Arthur King of Britain,* p. 328.

Page 18, "the general destruction": Jenkins, *The Mystery of King Arthur,* p. 22.

Page 19, "the legends . . . encouraged": James and Thorpe, *Ancient Mysteries,* p. 529.

Page 20, "sometime a famous" and "they have heard": Ashe, *The Discovery of King Arthur* p. 80.

Page 20, "somebody, clearly": James and Thorpe, *Ancient Mysteries,* p. 457.

Page 21, "HIC IACET SEPULTUS": Ashe, *The Discovery of King Arthur,* p. 175.

Chapter Four: The Saint and the Prince

Page 25, "a light boat" and "covered it": O'Meara, *The Voyage of Saint Brendan,* p. 8.

Page 25, "so numerous that": ibid., p. 15.

Page 25, "took what fruit": ibid., p. 67.

Page 28, "helped to demolish": Severin, *The Brendan Voyage,* p. 259.

Page 29, "Madoc was the outcast": Deacon, *Madoc and the Discovery of America,* p. 37.

Page 29, "left the land": Boland, *They All Discovered America,* p. 284.

Page 30, "after long saile": Deacon, *Madoc and the Discovery of America,* p. 182.

Page 31, "fortified some advantagious": ibid., p.182.

Page 31, "moon-eyed people": "Georgia's Ft. Mountain and Prince Madoc of Wales," p. 1.

Page 33, "had come from" and "knew better Welsh": Deacon, *Madoc and the Discovery of America,* p. 158.

Chapter Five: The Popess

Page 37, "two years" and "she became pregnant": Stanford, *The Legend of Pope Joan,* p. 19.

Page 38, "Pope John VIII": Editors of Reader's Digest, *Great Mysteries of the Past,* p. 295.

Page 39, "Despite all attempts" and "People believe in": Stanford, *The Legend of Pope Joan,* p. 182.

Chapter Six: The Outlaw

Page 41, "the most memorable": Bellamy, *Robin Hood,* p. i.

Page 42, "rymes of Robyn Hode": Editors of Reader's Digest, *Great Mysteries of the Past,* p. 286.

Page 42, "was a good outlawe": Holt, *Robin Hood,* p. 38.

Page 43, "the original and": Bellamy, *Robin Hood,* p. 35.

Page 43, "About this time": Knight, *Robin Hood,* p. 37.

Page 43, "Robert Fitzooth, commonly": ibid., p. 18.

Page 44, "Edwarde our comly kynge": Bellamy, *Robin Hood,* p. 9.

Page 45, "Now it will": James and Thorpe, *Ancient Mysteries,* p. 470.

Page 46, "troubled with sicknesse": Knight, *Robin Hood,* p. 40.

Page 46, "here lie[s]": ibid., p. 20.

Page 47, "could well embody": Holt, *Robin Hood,* p. 58.

Page 47, "the name originally": Knight, *Robin Hood,* p. 13.

Chapter Seven: The City of Gold

Page 49, "a few times": Editors of Time-Life Books, *The Search for El Dorado,* p. 10.

Page 50, "with a kind" and "make offerings": ibid., p.10.

Page 50, "Gold is . . . worshipped": Chapman, *The Search for El Dorado,* p. 91.

Page 54, "very white and tall": ibid., p. 107.

Page 55, "to honor my": ibid., p. 240.
Page 56, "I never knew": ibid., p. 239.

INDEX

**Page numbers for illustrations
are in boldface**

ABOUT THE AUTHOR

ABOUT THE AUTHOR

GARY L. BLACKWOOD has long been fascinated both with history and with the mysterious, so it's only natural that he should combine the two—not only in this set of books but in many of his other works, including the nonfiction series SECRETS OF THE UNEXPLAINED, and the historical novels *The Shakespeare Stealer, The Year of the Hangman,* and *Second Sight.*